WISDOM CLUES

SOCIAL WISDOM FOR AN UN-SOCIAL WORLD

JOHN S. ROLLINS

Published by MOTIV8U of North Central Florida, Inc.
Cover and interior design by Chernitra Palencia
Copyright © 2017 by John S. Rollins
For information on other materials:
MOTIV8U of North Central Florida
4600 NW 143rd Street
Gainesville, FL 32606
motiv8uofncf@gmail.com
Published in the United States of America

TABLE OF CONTENT

ACKNOWLEDGEMENTS

Social media has become an ever-present reality in our culture. It is from my participation in this communication explosion that the idea for this book surfaced. I have countless 'friends' online who have suggested that I should compile this material and offer it. A huge thank you to each one of you who have expressed an interest.

Katrina and MarQuelle, I am deeply grateful to you for your assistance in helping me smooth out the rough edges. This has been a long process and your patience is genuinely appreciated.

Nitra, I came to you because you are the best I know at what you do. Remember, the world is waiting for your unveiling.

To my family, thank you for allowing me to get 'lost' in thought for those periods. It is because of your belief in me that I continue to press toward a brighter tomorrow.

Father, thank you. You continue to amaze me. Where You lead, I will follow.

INTRODUCTION

A conversation between two friends may go something like this… "I have a surprise for you" the first person would say, with a huge smile on her face. "What is it?" asks the other person, nervously. "I can't tell you now but I am sure you are going to love it" replies the first person, intentionally adding to the anxiety. With increasing anticipation the exchange continues until the second person asks, "Well, can you give me a clue?"

From that exchange, the two individuals begin a game of Twenty Questions, going back and forth with a set of clues that may or may not bring any more light to the issue. Depending on the investigatory skills of the inquirer and the dismissiveness of the responder, the two could go back and forth without ever uncovering the surprise. However, if the clues are easily identifiable, most people would eventually discover the gift.

There are some people for whom it seems the dots connect more easily. Some call it intuition or insight. Others refer to it as some form of discernment. Regardless of what you call it, once these individuals hear the instructions; they are able to quickly apply what they have heard and learned and reap the benefits of their actions.

Christ said, *"Therefore whoever hears these sayings of Mine, and does them, I will liken him to a wise man who built his house on the rock: and the rain descended, the floods came, and the winds blew and beat on that house; and it did not fall, for it was founded on the rock. But everyone who hears these sayings of Mine, and does not do them, will be like a foolish man who built his house on the sand; and the rain descended, the floods came, and the winds blew and beat on that house; and it fell. And great was its fall."* Matthew 7:24-27 NKJV.

I have heard people say that life is hard; it is not fair and the journey becomes too difficult at times. While there may be some truth to this, I tend to disagree to some extent. Life, at its root, really isn't as unfair as some have asserted. Life may be hard and it may be difficult at times, but life does offer us choices. We have sole control of what we do with the information presented to us.

In *Wisdom Clues - Social Wisdom for an Unsocial World*, you will find practical insight for everyday living. Regardless of whether you are offered opportunities to relate with others or you are simply looking for an edge in your personal development, the information contained in this book provides you with wisdom from the ages that you can use to assist you in making your decision. You will be reminded that you have been given control, as well as the power that is needed, to shape your thoughts and actions.

Wisdom is looking at the current condition through the eyes of previous experiences and immutable truths (God's Word), considering possible outcomes or consequences and the impact on others and yourself, then making the decision that is most closely consistent with what is right. The voice of Wisdom is like the siren of a vehicle approaching an intersection, warning you so you can respond appropriately.

The winds blow on us all – winds of life, adversity, and opportunity. Some will see the effects of the wind and choose to close the shutters. They become paralyzed with fear and indecision. Others will see the wind and pull out the kites or set their sails. They will harness the wind to help propel them to the accomplishment of their goals. Which one will you CHOOSE to become?

Chapter 1
ACHIEVEMENT
WISDOM CLUES

Whoever watches the wind will not plant; whoever looks at the clouds will not reap. Sow your seed in the morning, and at evening let your hands not be idle, for you do not know which will succeed, whether this or that, or whether both will do equally well.
Ecclesiastes 11:4, 6 NIV

Seeds that remain in the bag will never produce a harvest. You will never score the winning point, graduate from college, close the major deal, or start a business if you never try. You should never expect to experience all that life has to offer if you refuse to get out of the stands and onto the playing field. Take the seeds out of the bag and plant them in good soil and prepare to receive your harvest.

If more of your time is spent in the stands or on the sideline watching than on the field playing, you may be living a 'Less-Than-Life'.

We have all been told that Wheaties is the breakfast of champions. If that is true, DISCIPLINE makes up their lunch, dinner, and snacks. The diet for those who continually succeed must include discipline!

To rise above and remain on top of the tide of mediocrity, talent, ability and giftedness alone will not suffice. Discipline is required, for it is through the furnace of discipline that talent, ability and giftedness is refined.

Harvest is a noun and a verb. In order to enjoy the benefits of the harvest one must be willing to work to reap it in its season. Fruit that is not removed *from* the vine typically dies *on* the vine.

When I commit to any venture I fully expect that some good will come of it. I don't control what my outcome will always be but I expect a positive outcome. If I continue to sow, at least one, and maybe more of my seeds will produce a harvest. And I can control how many seeds I put in the ground.

Great achievement is usually born of great sacrifice, and is never the result of selfishness. – Napoleon Hill

UNCOVERING THE CLUES

What are the factors that have contributed to your greatest achievements to date?

How can you take those success factors and transfer them to other areas of your life?

On a scale of 1 – 10, how disciplined are you?

What can you do to increase the level of your discipline?

Consider taking a chance on you. You may be surprised by the outcome.

You deserve a life of fulfillment. You've waited long enough.
Get started today.

Chapter 2
CHANGE
WISDOM CLUES

Who is like the wise? Who knows the explanation of things? A person's wisdom brightens their face and changes its hard appearance.
Ecclesiastes 8:1

On a clock that functions correctly, 2:00 will always come after 1:00. Our calendar always has Tuesday following after Monday. The sun always rises in the East and sets in the West. There are some things that are not designed to change and we do not have to pray about them. On the other hand, we have been afforded the privilege of changing - our looks, likes, locations and attitudes. Those are things about which we can pray.

When a person says they are ready for change, often the translation is they are ready for COMFORT. What they usually want is to go back to the place where it doesn't hurt as much. The truth is without change, going back to that comfortable place leaves them on the same road that gets them back to where they are now. In most cases, making positive changes require a level of discomfort, and sometimes pain - at least for a while.

So many people are still "Waiting to Exhale." In the literal sense, they hold oxygen-depleted air in their body. It no longer has value. By continuing to retain it they are closer to dying. It is similar in the spiritual. Holding on to things and people whose usefulness has expired is of no value to you. The longer you hold on, regardless of who or what it is, the greater the time delay in getting what you need to sustain you.

Someone else has overcome the obstacles that are confronting you.

Christ will not compete with your past. He erases it.

How many times have you realized that your comfort zone makes you very uncomfortable?

I find it interesting in life that for many people their biggest fear is change and the unknown. But there is another group of people that I've come across. For them their biggest fear is remaining the same.

Overcome to become.

When one spends more time questioning the motives of others than purifying their own they may be living a 'Less-Than-Life'.

Opportunity – an awareness that you can make a decision today that will change your future and make it drastically different from your past.

There are some things (and people) in your life that are nice but not necessary, while there are some that are necessary but not nice.

Change your style of living, improve your quality of life.

It is okay to occasionally visit your past but don't make it a practice to live there.

Our results, like a reflection from the mirror, reveal a picture of an accumulation of our actions and decisions. The mirror won't change the reflection any more than the results change the actions or decisions. The results, and the reflection, change when we do.

Progress is impossible without change, and those who cannot change their minds cannot change anything.
George Bernard Shaw

UNCOVERING THE CLUES

How convinced are you that by making some minor adjustments in your habits you will receive invaluable benefits?

What experiences from the past are you still holding on to today? Why?

What change(s) can you make today that will serve you best in the future?

Consider taking a chance on you. You may be surprised by the outcome.

You deserve a life of fulfillment. You've waited long enough. Get started today.

Chapter 3
CHARACTER/INTEGRITY
WISDOM CLUES

Do not be misled: Bad company corrupts good character.
1 Corinthians 15:33

How I live in this world will determine how I live in the next. It's been said that the best predictor of future performance is past performance. So, if I have character issues that have been problems for me in the past, and I have done nothing to address them, they will most likely surface in the future. If I am not careful, my habits may not only remain with me for my future but they may shape my future.

People can only give you what they have. It does not make sense to get upset with the employee at Burger King® when you cannot get a Big Mac®. In the same way, it is not wise to become frustrated by people who perform in a manner consistent with their character. When someone has consistently demonstrated flaws in their value system, we always have the choice to leave that situation and order from a different menu.

When my heart isn't right, my actions probably are not either. Many people do things outwardly but their heart (motive) is inconsistent with their actions. Paraphrasing the Scriptures, "...you worship me with your lips but your hearts are far from me." Maybe that's why the psalmist said, "Create in me a clean heart, O God, and renew a steadfast spirit within me." Psalms 51:10. Lord, purify my heart!

Identify as early as you can those things which, for you, are nonne-gotiable. Dr. Martin Luther King, Jr. said, "If a man doesn't stand for something, he will fall for anything." When we have and are guided by boundaries (values), instead of having to explain why we crossed them, we can celebrate the victories we achieve because we remained quali-fied for the race.

Being gifted at anything becomes irrelevant if you offend all the people who could benefit from your gift. Some people have a 'sandpaper' per-sonality and they create so much friction and conflict that others feel it is impossible to work effectively with them. Then there is the group who seems to make everything better by their presence. Successful people learn to build bridges, not barriers.

Don't be too hasty to defend yourself against LIES about your character.

Some people get pleasure out of creating strife and watching to see how others react to it. Many may choose to believe the lie, but it is in the truth where you are empowered. Christ remained silent concerning the lies spoken about Him. He knew the truth and spent His time educating others who were interested in the same.

Are you SOULED-out, SOLED-out, or SOLD-out? How can you tell the difference? SOULED-out people will do anything to advance their status, even if it costs them their soul. SOLED-out people have wearied and frustrated themselves by trying to do things on their own. SOLD-out people say, "My heart is fixed, my mind's made up. It doesn't matter anymore; I am going all the way with the Lord." Which one are you?

Some people are like thin ice. On the surface they appear stable. But under a little pressure they crack and shatter. Be careful of people who are all about appearances but have little substance. There was a fig tree, which under closer inspection, proved to be quite a disappointment. If you are putting your confidence in an image only, you may end up disappointed and your needs will remain unmet.

The loudest voice on matters of integrity is often one's track record. When you have earned respect for being a person of integrity, people accept your words. In many cases, there will be no need for an explanation; your past actions say it all. When your character is suspect, people's opinions of you are suspect also. In that case, telling the truth matters little because people may not believe you.

Often the greatest indication of one's strength is revealed in one's meekness.

In order to continually do good one has to be good. Most of us are familiar with someone who sprang up to fame and notoriety quickly, only to have sunk into obscurity and never be heard of again. Longevity typically results from a person who is good, being good at what he or she does.

I may be willing to apologize for what I do but not for who I am.

The greatest challenge of leadership is becoming someone that others want to follow.

RIGHT is its own validation.

Three things each person needs to know... 1. Who God is, 2. Who you are, and 3. Who your friends are.

Regardless of how long it has to endure the persistent and demanding pressure to change, RIGHT will never give in to wrong!

A companion of great responsibilities is great trials.

Sometimes, what you don't do speaks more accurately of your character.

A person can die of thirst in the midst of a rainstorm. So, also, can we die of sin when we are surrounded by the Word of God. The Apostle James said, "...be you doers of the word, not hearers only."

Maturity - Making decisions and taking actions which you are proud of at the time you make them AND still proud when you are questioned about them later.

As WITHIN, so WITHOUT.

Just because it may have gone unnoticed doesn't mean it went undone.

The true test of sincerity is more often the motives than the actions.

Men of genius are admired; men of wealth are envied; men of power are feared. But only men of character are trusted. Arthur Friedman

UNCOVERING THE CLUES

Which is of greater importance to you – your image or your character? Why?

Would you rather win or be right? Explain.

Of the three options – SOULED OUT, SOLED OUT, OR SOLD OUT, which one are you?

Consider taking a chance on you. You may be surprised by the outcome.

You deserve a life of fulfillment. You've waited long enough. Get started today.

Chapter 4
CHOICE
WISDOM CLUES

*If you must choose, take a good name rather than great riches; for to
be held in loving esteem is better than silver and gold.*
Proverbs 22:1 The Living Bible

Some people are happy about the sun only after the hurricane passes.
For them it seems nothing goes well. They find a problem in every opportunity. Only after enduring great calamity do they become apprecia-
tive – maybe. But every day brings something to smile about to those
who want to smile. This is the day the Lord has made and I CHOOSE to
rejoice and be glad in it.

The anchor is intended to hold the boat in place. Trying to move the boat
with the anchor in place can slow progress and cause significant damage. Are there things or people in our lives who slow our progress, and
significantly damage our potential? Pull up the anchor where possible.
If you can't pull it up, cut the rope and leave the anchor so you can move
forward.

When we tolerate something for so long it has a way of becoming OUR
norm. Because we tolerate it, we often tie our own hands and therefore
jeopardize our right to complain about it. The changes we want to see
in our lives cannot coexist with the things we do not want or like but
continue to tolerate.

It is highly unlikely that you will find RESPONSIBILITY and EXCUS-
ES to be traveling companions on any trip worth taking. Some people
get while others give. You have those people who get results and you
have those people who give excuses as to why they did not obtain results. YOU can choose which type person you want to become.

Everything I have learned to value has come at a cost. Many times I
have been willing to pay the price and set something aside. Other times,
the cost was garnished from my wages and taken, whether I wanted to
pay or not. What it taught me to do was spend more time counting the
cost before I make my decisions. At least, I now have some idea how
much to prepare to spend.

In every situation you have a choice. The options before you may not
be the most attractive but in most cases you have more than one. When
the first option is least desirable, review the facts of the others. Then

15

go to the NBA (Next Best Alternative.) Often, in the absence of all the facts, do as much research as you can and then act in faith – trusting & believing that all things work together for good –for you.

Belief does not and should not hinge upon understanding. There are many things we believe but may never understand. Many will never understand how and why the body's core temperature must remain within a certain range. Few can explain how the brain needs blood, but why too much blood on the brain can cause traumatic outcomes. I don't understand why a Holy God offers salvation to all, but I surely believe.

The issue isn't how will God respond to us but how will we respond to Him. Will you say "Yes?" God said, "I am the Lord God, and I change not." Often, we continue doing things that don't work; asking God to change. The wise thing to do is to find out what we are doing that is not working, stop doing it, and get on board with a system that will not fail. God's system is fool proof and 'foolish' proof. Do it His way.

Whether for good or bad, for something positive or negative, our minds will always see more than our eyes. Whenever there is something that frightens us or that we don't want to see, we can voluntarily close our eyes or turn our heads. Similarly, whenever there are negative things that potentially destroy our ambitions and dreams, we can close our mind and shut it out. Thankfully, we alone control how much and often we keep our minds open.

Often, the level of greatness one achieves is proportionate to the level of trials one is willing to endure. Winners and achievers are the individuals willing to stay the course and endure pain and discomfort. They persist, despite the frustrations and disappointments.

Hard Times is an unwelcomed guest who often comes unannounced to all - people, residences and businesses. However, I can choose to not offer him an extended stay or long-term lease agreement.

Someone might say, "My instincts tell me ..." It is so important to learn how to appropriately respond to that still, small voice that speaks to us.

So many people are choosing to become what they were never meant to be.

Every opportunity comes with an expiration date.

TIME. You can waste it, you can spend it, you can invest it, but you cannot stop it and you cannot get it back.

Opportunity will come, but normally unannounced. Be prepared.

Distance yourself from the things and the people that routinely frustrate you.

The mind can be bound only with permission.

Half of the battle is knowing what you want. The other half is knowing what you do not want. I want to go to heaven. I do not want to go to hell.

Your world will be ruled by thoughts. It will either be ruled by someone else's thoughts or your own.

Being THANKFUL is something I choose to do.

Plan A - Trust in the Lord with all your heart and lean not on your own understanding. Plan B - Defer to Plan A.

Half of an open mind is better than a whole closed mind.

One's philosophy is not best expressed in words; it is expressed in the choices one makes... and the choices we make are ultimately our responsibility. Eleanor Roosevelt

UNCOVERING THE CLUES

On a scale of 1-10, with 10 being 'Fantastic', how would you rate your choices over the past year?

Are you known more for helping others to choose or for getting others to help you choose?

Where and how do you spend most of your time? Your money? Your energy? Your choices in these areas reveal your priorities.

Consider taking a chance on you. You may be surprised by the outcome.

You deserve a life of fulfillment. You've waited long enough. Get started today.

Chapter 5
COMMUNICATION
WISDOM CLUES

Do not let any unwholesome talk come out of your mouths, but only what is helpful for building others up according to their needs, that it may benefit those who listen. Ephesians 4:29 NIV

If there was a price tag for your listening skills would you receive money or have to pay? Some people hear but not many people take time to listen. Why? It takes effort. Listening requires that we slow down and direct attention to others. When we are convinced we are right, we are not as interested in hearing input from others. Smart people know what they know but wise people also listen to learn from others.

People will hear what they want to hear (regardless of what was actually said) and believe what they want to believe (regardless of whether or not it is the truth).

According to the Bible, the heart is connected to the tongue.

Whether you believe it or not, you will listen to YOU more than you listen to anyone else.

Quit spending so much time focusing on "who" is doing the talking and spend more time focusing on "what" is being said.

Opinions are much like discounted objects at a garage sale. You can get a lot of them for little to nothing. In most cases, the person giving the opinion feels like it is worth a lot more than the person receiving it. However, there will be some occasions when you come across an opinion that is far more valuable to you than any price you could have paid.

Take flying lessons from the bird, not the fish. Before you allow someone to pour into your life, at least make sure the individual is good at what he or she does.

Be careful of people who always question other's motives. Some questioned the woman who poured her fragrance on the Master, saying more could have been done with it. In reality, they were the ones who were in need of more - more of Him. Maybe instead of getting upset with them, we should pray for them.

Unless you are surrounded by mirrors you can only see one side of what others see. Wise people seek and listen to feedback. Do people tell you things to try to save you from embarrassment? Is there toilet paper on your shoes or is your skirt tucked in your panty hose? Trusted friends (or children) can tell us things about ourselves that we may not know. When they do, learn to accept it with gratitude.

Who, or what, is it that you use as the standard for judging yourself?

The bridge covering some of the pitfalls of life is made up of the backs of people who fell into the pit. Instead of moving them out of the way and falling yourself, ask for their permission and use their backs to successfully cross over.

Take advantage of every opportunity to practice your communication skills so that when important occasions arise, you will have the gift, the style, the sharpness, the clarity, and the emotions to affect other people. Jim Rohn

UNCOVERING THE CLUES

When surrounded by people which do you do most, talk or listen?

How much time do you spend doing research on a topic before giving your opinion?

What is the content of most of your 'self-talk'? Do you need to make changes?

Consider taking a chance on you. You may be surprised by the outcome.

You deserve a life of fulfillment. You've waited long enough.
Get started today.

Chapter 6

DECISIONS
WISDOM CLUES

Death is the reward of an undisciplined life; your foolish decisions trap you in a dead end. Proverbs 5:23 The Message

The longer you remain on the wall, the more likely you will fall. Just ask Humpty Dumpty. The wall represents indecision. In the Bible, the Apostle James said the person who is double minded is unstable in all his ways. Both sides may have attractive options. Weigh the pros and cons and then make a decision. Get off the wall and into the Well – the Well of Water springing up to everlasting life.

An HONEST evaluation of our current situations will reveal that OUR decisions have been a primary contributor to where we are today. There were things that happened to us that were beyond our control. For other outcomes, we were solely responsible. Not much can be done to undo what occurred in the past. However, we are in a good position to begin shaping our future. We create our best future by making better decisions today.

Live and learn. The statement suggests the longer we live, the more we should have learned. So what does it mean when we are still repeating some of the same behaviors; making the same mistakes this year as we did in the past? Are we learning? My take – I only consider errors a mistake if I don't learn from them. When I learn from them AND eliminate repeat occurrences it was a valuable life lesson.

What are you doing with that which has been given to you? You are not expected to produce with the gifts or talents of another. Neither is it expected that you sit on the talents you receive. Each of us possesses something we can use, which will in turn produce more. When you are judged it will be based on how you performed using that with which you were provided. Use what you have.

When we quit stopping ourselves, there are not many other things that can stop us!

It is of little value to be in the right place at the right time and do the wrong thing. When we learn to take advantage of those seasons we enjoy our greatest harvest.

If your past decisions were a banquet, what would be on the menu for today?

Imagine what a difference there would be if we would use common sense as much as we used the other natural resources.

So many people are still taking things into their TOMORROW that they did not like or want TODAY!

The biggest adversary that most will have to overcome is their OWN ignorance.

How likely are we to DO what Jesus did if we do not THINK like Jesus thought?

If I knew the full impact of my next decision would I still make it?

Thank God for a future not limited by my failures.

Solutions to some of the biggest challenges are often found in the doing the simplest things.

Where I am does not define who I am!

Procrastination is the enemy of opportunity!

In any moment of decision, the best thing you can do is the right thing, the next best thing is the wrong thing, and the worst thing you can do is nothing. Theodore Roosevelt

UNCOVERING THE CLUES

Do you make decisions quickly or does it take a long time?

Once you have made a decision, how easily do you change your mind?

How you do handle it when you discover you have made the wrong decision?

Consider taking a chance on you. You may be surprised by the outcome.

You deserve a life of fulfillment. You've waited long enough. Get started today.

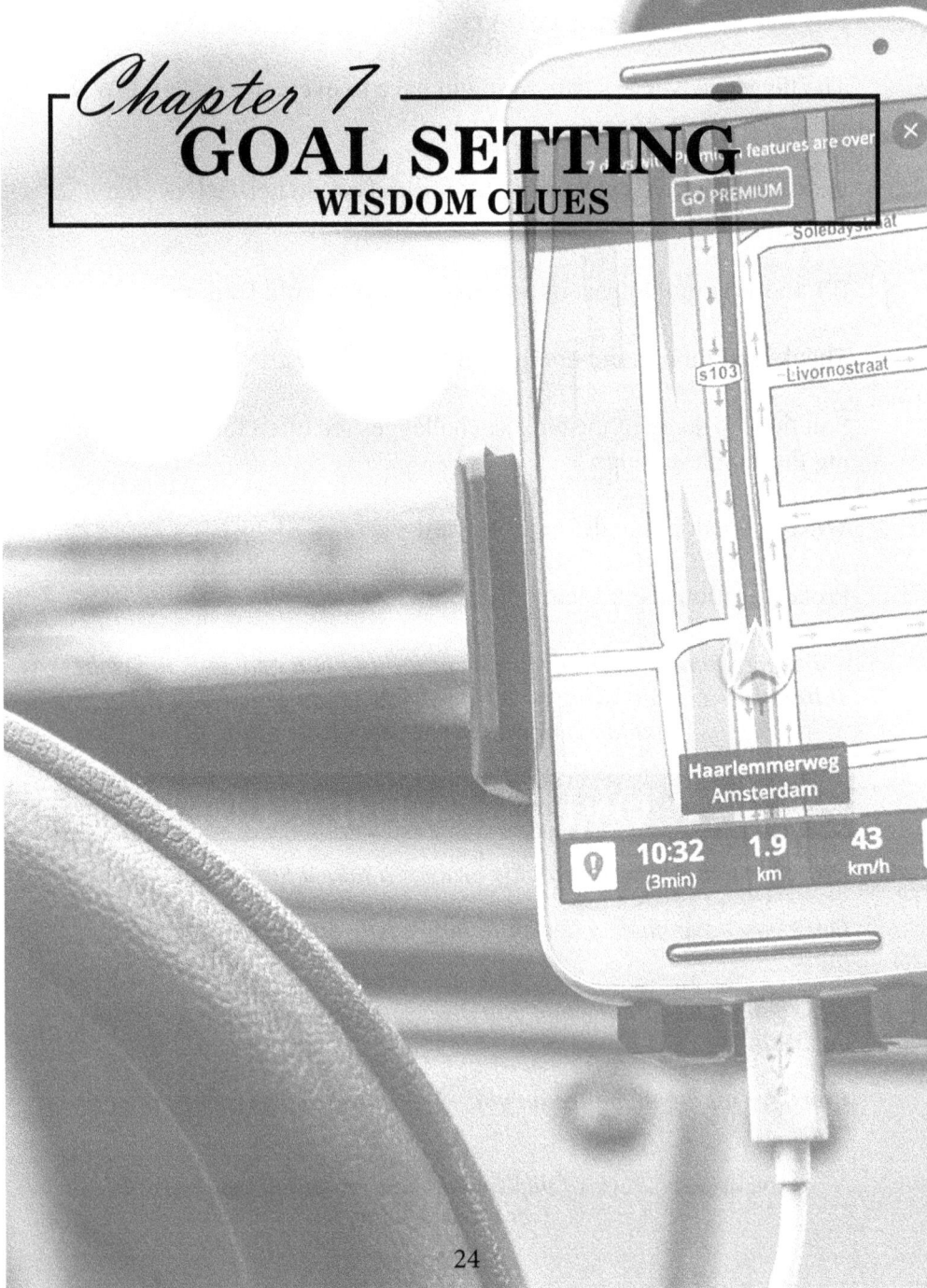

Chapter 7
GOAL SETTING
WISDOM CLUES

Have two goals: wisdom—that is, knowing and doing right—and common sense. Don't let them slip away, for they fill you with living energy and bring you honor and respect. Proverbs 3:21-22 The Living Bible

When travelling, don't set your destination by using the GPS of the car next to you. Although the satellite systems may be the same, the destination is most likely different. The other occupants may arrive at their location long before you do. In life, it is not a good idea to determine your success or failure based on someone else's journey. Follow the road map leading you to where you are supposed to go.

Sometimes you will have traveled too far toward your destination to consider turning around or stopping. Maybe you left something you thought you needed. But after going so far on the journey you have determined that it wouldn't make sense to turn around now. Rev. James Cleveland said, "'I've come too far from where I started from." Keep going - you're closer than you think!

A GOAL mind is a GOLD mine. People who consistently land in the upper percentile for finances and accomplishments are individuals who've learned the art of setting and achieving their goals. They have well thought-out goals that they've committed to paper and shared with an accountability partner. Whenever obstacles arise, they understand the goal is one worth fighting for and they press forward.

Avoid dream-stealers like you would avoid the plague. It is a crime to steal property: a purse, car, even livestock. It can deprive one of his/her livelihood. It should be an equally serious offense to steal a person's dream. One of the greatest gifts given to humanity by the Creator is the ability to dream - not just with your eyes closed. Resolve to chase after your dreams and NEVER allow anyone to steal them!

The reason so many people are afraid to make demands on life is because they do not know their rights! America's citizens have specific inalienable rights available to us simply because of our birth place. For those of us who are Kingdom citizens, we, too, have certain rights. I am not to blame anyone for not explaining to me what's rightfully mine. I am to learn, walk in, and demand that which belongs to me.

We are fortunate who understand that the struggle is not to keep us where we are. The struggle is to keep us from where we are going. Too often we spend our time fighting minor battles when the outcome we really seek is to be victorious in the war. Keep your focus on the goal, not the position.

Sometimes you will not know where you are supposed to go until you are rejected where you are!

Regardless of the destination, the path is seldom straight and the road is seldom smooth.

Here is a sign that one is living the 'Less-Than-Life'... When a person wants what someone else has but is unwilling to do what they did to get it.

Too often, that which is attained too easily is esteemed too lightly.

It is a whole lot easier (and faster) to go to the snail than to wait for the snail to come to you. Are you waiting for your dreams, words of prophecy, or promises to be fulfilled or are you pursuing them? "Do not merely desire peaceful relations with God,… and with yourself, but pursue, go after it!" 1 Peter 3:11b AMP. The snail may come, but it probably won't be any time soon.

> *The poor man is not he who is without a cent, but he*
> *who is without a dream.*
> Harry Kemp

UNCOVERING THE CLUES

When setting goals, do you make them Specific, Measurable, Attainable, Realistic, with a Timeline (S.M.A.R.T.)?

What is one goal that, if you were to accomplish it, would have the greatest positive impact on your life this year?

What has been your most effective technique for reaching your goals?

What are you willing to go through to get you where you want to be?

Consider taking a chance on you. You may be surprised by the outcome.

You deserve a life of fulfillment. You've waited long enough.
Get started today.

Chapter 8

LOVE
WISDOM CLUES

The man who tries to be good, loving, and kind finds life, righteousness, and honor. Proverbs 21:21 The Living Bible

Love is a powerful weapon. Lives have been started and ended because of love. A great preacher once wrote, "I Did It In the Name of Love." Love, properly appropriated, removes emotions, thoughts, and selfishness from the equation and often responds in spite of. In order to get to that place, we can't just be in love. Love has to be in us – we become love. That is why God is able to give and forgive. He is Love.

Love must feed on LOVE.

Love.... First!

Lord, grant me that I may lovingly gaze upon others through the lens of compassion through which You lovingly gaze upon me.

It is my belief that the persons who are willing to love the deepest are the ones able to live to the fullest.

Motes and Beams - Often we want to remove the motes of others with an axe while we want others to remove our beams with tissues.
Which is usually easier - to find fault with another or to find fault within?

Many people will TELL you how good a friend they are to you. It's when things get rough that you find out who is telling the truth.

Love allows for the imperfections of others. Criticism can make friends avoid each other.

If we only knew how many people were touched by our smile we would frown less. Things don't always work out the way we want. Maybe it's best that way. The diamond needs pressure to form. Gold needs fire for refining. After enduring and overcoming the struggle, the caterpillar emerges with beautiful wings. If it's not quite how you want it to be, it's probably better than it could be. Keep smiling.

In life we can be full of cares or we can be full of care.

"Your career is what you are paid for; your calling is what you are made for." - Dr. Howard Hendricks

A life lived in service to others is one that is most fulfilling. Twenty-four hours from now, what will you have done that will have made someone else's life better? Others can benefit from your smile or touch. You can share an encouraging word with someone or simply give them your attention. The reward may appear small at the time, but YOUR actions may be just the inspiration someone needs today. Serve-Love-Live.

I encourage everyone to get vaccinated this year with their F.L.U. shot... FORGIVENESS - LOVE - UNDERSTANDING. It will help prevent many people from becoming sick.

Is it possible that one born among you, living among you, working among you, could have been chosen to bring a blessing and revelation to you? Are you willing to be the one chosen to bring a blessing and revelation to another?

When it's all said and done, the one question by which I strive to govern my life is, "Will I be counted worthy of the kingdom of heaven?"

Don't live to IMPRESS. Live to IMPACT!

My LIFE is the witness that Jesus won the total victory.

Your maturity in certain areas of your life better enable you to understand the immaturity of others in areas of their lives.

You can give without loving, but you cannot love without giving.
-Mark Graham

UNCOVERING THE CLUES

What do you think of when you hear the phrase 'unconditional love'?

When is it most difficult for you to express love?

When is it easiest for you to express love?

Are you more likely to love the person or what the person does?

Consider taking a chance on you. You may be surprised by the out come.

You deserve a life of fulfillment. You've waited long enough.
Get started today.

Chapter 9

PERSONAL GROWTH
WISDOM CLUES

But if you correct those who care about life, that's different—they'll love you for it! Save your breath for the wise—they'll be wiser for it; tell good people what you know—they'll profit from it.
Proverbs 9:8-9 The Message

What we were yesterday is not what we have to be today. How many people have individuals who remember how we were while we were still being developed? The only image they have of us is based on the person we used to be. They have formed a picture in their minds of who we are today, based on who we were then. During the development stages we were of little value to anyone. To them, we are still eggs, butter, flour, salt, and flavoring. We experienced painful and unpleasant moments – times when we were broken, beaten and whipped. But, thank God, He has taken those ingredients, all those moments, all those experiences, to form us into a beautiful cake.

We will never consistently exceed beyond our capacity. Most people desire more but many have not committed to the activities that deserve more. In order for us to get a 'boatload' of anything, regardless of what it may be, wouldn't it make sense to first get a boat? As we expand our capacity, we expand our opportunity.

We need to cast our cares where God casts our sins. When He is done with them, the Scriptures tell us He remembers them no more. Wouldn't it be nice to have forgotten exactly what it was that you were worried about and that consumed you?

We have filters in our cars, in our A/C's and on our appliances. Why? They are there to protect the investment and keep it functioning at a premium. Wouldn't it make sense to put a filter on our minds and our hearts? After all, what greater investment is there? When not filtered, we may be allowing pollutants in that are damaging our very being.

Identity theft is one of the fastest growing crimes. Has the enemy stolen your identity or did you just let him borrow it? When the enemy stole King David's possessions and his men turned on him, God told him to go and get his stuff - recover all. Take back your identity from the enemy and live in abundance.

33

There is only one manual that addresses and can fix all makes and models. Ford, Samsung, Maytag only address problems with their specific equipment. The Holy Bible addresses and can fix problems with ANY of us. "I am the Lord, the God of all mankind. Is anything too hard for Me?" Jer.32:27. I don't know about you, but I am checking my manual.

Sow mercy in abundance. That way, when the time comes wherein we need some, there will be enough to meet our need. And we will still have some to spare.

To stay ahead of the game, you have to renew YOURSELF. Stephen Covey called it 'Sharpening the saw.' Some people are trying to function on a daily basis wearing shoes or clothes that are 2-3 sizes too small. They are living their lives today based on how things once were. Others understand that the old has gone and they have to embrace something new. If you find that your feet hurt maybe your shoes are too small and perhaps it's time to let some things go. Renewal + Restoration could = Reward.

Here are 3 T's that can literally change your life: Tools, Training, and Time. Tools are designed to facilitate (make easier) the completion of the tasks. Training is necessary for you to improve your skills with the tools. Time is required to allow for the full realization of that for which you have prepared. By the way, it works to your advantage if you have the fourth T - Talent.

You are a survivor when you not only endure the shipwreck but use some of the broken pieces to help you get to shore. You will experience things that are intended to destroy you. Others counted you out. How surprised they were to see you when you came through. Although everything seemed lost, you were able to find something you could hold onto and you made it to the other side. Here's to the survivors.

Where do you focus most of your attention... On who you were, who you are or who you are created to be?

Growth is the great separator between those who succeed and those who do not. When I see a person beginning to separate themselves from the pack, it's almost always due to personal growth.
John C. Maxwell

UNCOVERING THE CLUES

What are some things from the past, people, experiences, successes or failures that you are refusing to let go?

How much time do you devote to thinking about your future?

What traits do you attribute to the people that you know who are 'survivors'? Which of these traits do you possess?

In what area(s) have you experienced the most growth this year?

What has contributed most to this growth?

Consider taking a chance on you. You may be surprised by the out come.

You deserve a life of fulfillment. You've waited long enough. Get started today.

Chapter 10
PERSPECTIVE
WISDOM CLUES

Don't shuffle along, eyes to the ground, absorbed with the things right in front of you. Look up, and be alert to what is going on around Christ—that's where the action is. See things from his perspective. Colossians 3:2 The Message

Many people can look into my eyes, but I am the only one who can look through my eyes. I have sole control of what and how I see things. As much as I desire to make sure people see things as I do, they truly can't. I can only hope the people around me care enough to make the effort to try to understand me, while I try to understand others.

Many people would consider it an upgrade to be in the place where you are unhappy. Imagine how many people would love to be able to get up and go to work today but can't. Countless people would give anything to be in a relationship with someone with whom they can disagree. Leftovers mean there was something left. Thank You Lord for what I have and where I am.

Once you have overcome your opposition, the person or people you continue to attack may be your ally. Hurting people hurt people. People who survive "war-like" situations, whether at work, home or church, tend to keep up their defenses, and at times, even attack people who care about them. You may still have to keep your guard up, but survey the surroundings thoroughly to make sure you are not attacking people who are on your side.

Strive to know the difference between that which is a practice and that which is a law. People exercise practices thinking it is law. Other people violate laws thinking it is practice. If you continually choose not to shower, although it may be offensive, it is not illegal. However, breaking universal laws (of any kind) can be offensive and carry grave consequences.

Celebrate the YOU-niqueness that is you. Of all of the people on the earth, those who have gone before and those who will come after, none will ever be just like you. It is a testament to the value you possess. Each of your experiences, each of your exposures has harmoniously worked to create the wonderful person that you are. You are the best you to ever grace this earth. Someone's life has been enriched by you.

How would you live your life differently if you could get a glimpse of the greatness that others see in you?

For many, it appears your reality is unreal; your normal is abnormal. Does it look as though your path is full of briars, thorns and weeds? If you are poor in spirit, a mourner, or meek, I have good news. Christ said you are 'Blessed.' He said when you are persecuted for righteousness sake you receive the kingdom of heaven. Remain committed – do not quit. Many times, that which looks like dysfunction is in actuality His function.

Of all the things that can possibly hold me in bondage, nothing can hold me as strongly as my mind. No one would argue the power of an addiction, suggestion or fear. However, each of us has been equipped, emphasis on 'HAS BEEN', to overcome any stronghold. My body follows my mind. The battle is often won and my victory comes when I choose to be free! I CAN – I WILL – I HAVE OVERCOME.

If people get on your LAST nerve, what did you allow to happen to all of the other nerves? Had you eliminated all, or at least some of the other things that bothered you before you were down to the last one, maybe you could have preserved and protected the last one. We never want to allow anyone or anything to get us down to the very last one, because when the last one is gone, it's called extinction.

One thing that often challenges us is fighting the temptation to believe that the level from which we view things is the only level there is. Things created by God, including humanity, have multiple levels. A closed mind to other levels is like going through life believing that ground transportation is the only means of travel. But to the person looking out the window of the airplane, the view is completely different.

The eagle, majestic and powerful, and the bumblebee, awkward and clumsy, both fly. Often we celebrate, and at times, envy the person who is a natural. Some possess, through no efforts of their own, beauty, grace, talent, and stature. It's called genetics. Others, born without the same DNA, have achieved similar accomplishments, but had to overcome severe challenges and obstacles. They, too, deserve recognition.

The person or thing in your life that irritates you the most may have been placed there to produce your greatest value. An oyster, with no irritation or inconvenience, produces no pearl. It is purchased, cracked open and consumed for pennies in comparison to the price of the pearl. With the right perspective, our problem people and situations may actually be used to develop our true greatness.

It is amazing. When one changes his or her attitude toward the world the world changes its attitude toward the individual.

How would your life be if you had your way with it? And then how would your life be if God had His way with it?

For every problem, there is a solution.

If you are drowning your best friend may not be the person who jumps in the water with you. Your best friend maybe the person who stays on the bank and throws you a rope to pull you out of the drowning situation.

Almost anything can look good in bad lighting.

All of the people who come into our lives fulfill a purpose. Some of them provide us with the rain; others provide us with sunshine. Then there is the group who provides us with the dirt. Each one of them has their own role in helping us to grow.

Don't be too disappointed if the people in your life who were the first to 'buy-in' are also the ones who are the first to 'sell out.'

Time has no effect on truth except to reveal it.

It is highly unlikely that we are ever as good or as bad as how we picture ourselves in our mind.-

You must look within for value, but must look beyond for perspective.
                                                                    - Denis Waitley

UNCOVERING THE CLUES

Who can you depend on to help keep you grounded?

How do you balance entertaining facts versus opinion?

If everyone in your life fulfills a purpose, how do you differentiate between those supplying the sun, rain, and dirt?

Consider taking a chance on you. You may be surprised by the outcome.

You deserve a life of fulfillment. You've waited long enough.
Get started today.

40

Chapter 11

PLANNING/PREPARATION
WISDOM CLUES

Refuse good advice and watch your plans fail; take good counsel and watch them succeed. Proverbs 15:22 The Message

The best time to dig for water is before the drought. On the road for the family vacation is a bad time to discover the spare tire has no air. Many times we will be confronted with situations that we would not have anticipated. Other times we could have checked but did not or we simply ignored the signs. The light on the fuel gauge is there for a reason. Paranoia can be discomforting – ignorance, however, can be dangerous.

Too many people are defeated not because things got hard but because they had no plan of action for when hard times came. We don't mind unfortunate circumstances as much when we have an emergency plan and have prepared for it. I like my chances jumping out of the plane much better when I have a parachute and I have been trained how to use it. The greatest success comes when there is a succession plan.

The first item on my new 'To-Do' list is to create a 'Stop Doing' list. Proper preparation always provides an appropriate return.

More often than not, the thin line that defines successful and unsuccessful ventures is the plan.

Too often people believe that fate seems to control the destiny of so many. The reality, however, is that those people with a plan seem to control their own fate.

It takes a lot of time and effort to work through all of the details to come up with a good plan. It takes a lot more time and effort to redo the work that was done poorly as a result of someone refusing to properly plan.

Let our advance worrying become advance thinking and planning.
- Winston Churchill

UNCOVERING THE CLUES

How much time do you devote to developing a plan for your future?

Who are the people you know who can help you create a sound action plan for you for the next six months?

Are you more inclined to plan or to procrastinate? Why?

In the Goal Setting/Attainment section, you were asked, "What is one goal that, if you were to accomplish it, would have the greatest positive impact on your life this year?" What two things can/will you do this week toward that goal?

Consider taking a chance on you. You may be surprised by the outcome.

You deserve a life of fulfillment. You've waited long enough.
Get started today.

Chapter 12

PRAYER
WISDOM CLUES

Then Jesus told them, "Truly, if you have faith and don't doubt, you can do things like this and much more. You can even say to this Mount of Olives, 'Move over into the ocean,' and it will. You can get anything—anything you ask for in prayer—if you believe.
Matthew 21:21-22 TLB

God will tell you NO. It is consistent with His character. He told Moses and Abraham no. He told David and Paul no. Even for Christ's request there was but one way. We may ask God to grant us a request that is our DESIRE and not get the response we seek. Understand, our requests may get a no, but "…ALL the promises of God in Him are Yes and in Him amen." 2 Cor. 1:20 NKJV. Want better results? Pray His promises.

Often the topic comes up about whether prayer should be allowed in school. No one should be able to legislate when and where one is permitted to pray. Instead of trying to get prayer back in school, we become more effective when we make prayer a priority at home. If more people prayed at home, there would be fewer issues at school. For some of us prayer is not only a right but a responsibility and a requirement.

The Gospel of Jesus Christ - Plastic surgery for the heart.

Is there anyone else out there who is willing to confess to just how MESSED UP you were? .....But GOD.... The dots before speak to what you were before God. The dots after speak to what you are to become with God!

The real key to God's promises is.... GOD.

The outcome of sin is weightier than the act of sin. But God's forgiveness is greater. He said, "Go, and sin no more."

You can let God do it or God can let you do it. Hmmmmm. Which outcome do you think works best?

"There are three answers to prayer – Yes, No, and Wait." - Unknown

UNCOVERING THE CLUES

What do you think is the secret to answered prayer?

What or whom do you pray about most often?

When you pray, do you normally follow up with action?

If required, how comfortable are you with an answer of "No"?

Consider taking a chance on you. You may be surprised by the outcome.

You deserve a life of fulfillment. You've waited long enough. Get started today.

Chapter 13
SUCCESS
WISDOM CLUES

He who loves wisdom loves his own best interest and will be a success. Proverbs 19:8 The Living Bible

"It is easier to go from failure to success than it is to go from excuses to success." ~Unknown

Success comes in the valley, not on the mountaintop. On the mountain we celebrate our accomplishments, but it is in the valley where success is attained. In the valley battles are toughest, missteps are magnified and attitudes and actions are critical. But in the valley we have a partner who has promised to never leave nor forsake us. In Him we are over-comers and victorious. With Him we walk successfully.

Success leaves clues. Have you ever noticed that successful people hang around other successful people? I have come to understand that success leaves a trail of clearly, distinguishable prints that can be discovered by the eye that is trained to find them. Success, like money, happiness, and most of the other things we have come to appreciate, has no favorites. It will come to anyone and everyone who follows the clues.

It is the content of your past failures that has been ground up and used to create the fertilizer for your future success.

Success will not attack you!

People join commitment and follow courage.

Dreams are still available for free.

I am worthy of where I want to be.

No person who has achieved long-term success in any endeavor has done so without overcoming what appeared to be temporary defeat.

On this you can be sure ... anything that is limiting you was not placed there by God.

> *"I have learned that success is to be measured not so much by the position that one has reached in life as by the obstacles which he has overcome while trying to succeed."* Booker T. Washington

UNCOVERING THE CLUES

What brings you peace of mind and contentment?

How do you define success?

Who are others that can help contribute to your success?

What is your biggest fear or concern about experiencing success?

Consider taking a chance on you. You may be surprised by the outcome.

You deserve a life of fulfillment. You've waited long enough.
Get started today.

Chapter 14
WORK ETHIC
WISDOM CLUES

Observe people who are good at their work— skilled workers are always in demand and admired; they don't take a backseat to anyone.
Proverbs 22:29 The Message

"O Lord, thou givest us everything, at the price of an effort." - Leonardo Da Vinci

There is immense value in taking initiative. Many people are promoted because they are willing to do things no one else will. Remember David, the shepherd? When every other member of the king's army hid in fear, David took it upon himself to go out and defeat Goliath. Later, he was promoted to king. And it was through his lineage that the Savior of the world would come. Go ahead. Show some initiative.

If you are a giant slayer you owe no one an apology. Giant slayers are problem solvers. You have the fortitude, wisdom, and gift to look at problems that paralyze others and bring resolution. And you understand, like Joseph, that God gives the insight. He has been preparing you, like Esther, for such a time as this. Apologize? I am praising all day long!

Can you maintain what you attain? Can what you attain sustain you? The mosquito can conceive and hatch in 90 days and can be dead just as quickly. The elephant takes 12 months to deliver and can live for decades. When we commit to labor for something, let us labor for fruit that remains.

A FULL tank of gas with an engine that is running but in Park will get you no farther than if you had no gas at all. The greater benefit is realized when you not only possess things that achieve greatness, but do something with them. The Psalmist wrote, "...and he shall be like a tree that brings forth its fruit in its season and whatsoever he DO shall prosper." It sounds like some action is required on your part.

People are less interested in hearing your admission and/or alibi. People want to see evidence. Do not say what you are going to do unless your actions support it. A person can form their mouth to say anything. Evidence, on the other hand, says one thing – what you did or did not do. Produce a degree, paycheck, acceptance letter, pregnancy test or something that lets people know that you are not just talking.

Simple is not always easy. Without significant effort, things won't just fall in place. Things that are easy generally do not yield a great return. Many people rise to the top of their field or profession because they work hard; laboring long hours to improve their skills and knowledge. Their benefit is that they make the complicated look easy. The reality is that it was difficult long before it became easy.

In life some will receive a certificate of attendance with their name on a piece of paper indicating they were present. Others will receive a certificate of completion, having participated in the activities but were unsuccessful in the tests and get no credit for their work. Only those who earn a graduation diploma are recognized as having satisfactorily met all the requirements and are qualified to go to the next level.

One of the biggest gaps to overcome is the KNOWING-DOING gap. Too often we fail to act on that which we know to do. Most can recall a time when we did not follow up on something that needed to be done when it needed to be done. We knew what should be done but, regardless of the reason, we didn't do it. Opportunities abound. Those who seize them have reduced the space between what they know and what they do.

Although others can observe us and evaluate our actions, as well as our intentions, we are the only ones who can HONESTLY answer the question, "Did I give it my very best?" When we don't give our best, we are left to wonder what would have happened had we expended a little more effort. The difference between ORDINARY and extra-ORDINARY is that little extra. Instead of giving 110% once, consider giving 1% more in each effort.

My 'Dos' will overcome my 'DOUBTs'.

The promises of God are offered to everyone but not everyone is willing to do what's necessary to receive them.

There are not many forfeited victories in spiritual warfare.

If one is to be crowned champion, it means that s/he has engaged in battle or conflict and prevailed over his/her adversaries.

Your work is going to fill a large part of your life, and the only way to be truly satisfied is to do what you believe is great work. And the only way to do great work is to love what you do. If you haven't found it yet, keep looking. Don't settle. As with all matters of the heart, you'll know when you find it. – Steve Jobs

UNCOVERING THE CLUES

What has been one of the greatest accomplishments up to this point in your career?

How balanced is your work and personal life?

When undertaking a project, are you more interested in doing your part or making sure the team wins?

Consider taking a chance on you. You may be surprised by the outcome.

You deserve a life of fulfillment. You've waited long enough. Get started today.

www.ingramcontent.com/pod-product-compliance
Lightning Source LLC
Chambersburg PA
CBHW071434040426
42445CB00012BA/1361